Divinity Rising

"We are blessed when a genuine mystic answers the call to put his experiences into words. John's new book of poetry is a great gift to us all—but it is John, himself, who is the greatest gift."

—**Carol Orsborn**, author of *Spiritual Aging: Weekly Reflections for Embracing Life*

"John Robinson's *Divinity Rising: Beyond Illusion, Suffering and Death* is a tour de force necessary for our times. As I laughed and cried, the poetry kept calling me back to a deeper experience of the God within. Since humanity often yearns throughout history for external solutions, Dr. Robinson reminds that the real solutions are rooted in a deep sense of God's presence within each one of us. *Divinity Rising* is a work that should be on everyone's nightstand because it provides hope and inspiration for the creation of a world that would make God proud."

—**James L. Broderick**, author of *History of Psychology through Symbols*

"T.S. Eliot said, 'We shall not cease from exploration until we arrive at the place where we started and know the place for the first time.' *Divinity Rising* is the book to guide us. Our culture constantly urges us to explore and learn more, until we're drowning in travel and lifelong learning. But we should be looking for who will guide us to know where we are, where we started, and where we should go. John Robinson can be our guide. *Divinity Rising* offers poetry and a spiritual map beyond illusion and suffering."

—**Harry Moody**, author of *The Five Stages of the Soul: Charting the Spiritual Passages that Shape Our Lives*

"I love John's work. He has gone beyond the classic to the mystic—and that makes all the difference. Mystical poetry is the embodiment of the crazy wisdom that lies beyond the ordinary mind, in the realm of the God spark. It is a speaking from that realm of being drenched in Spirit. As John says in the opening pages, this is not a job or something you do for money. This is a gift given to rare ones, and if it breaks the heart open, then the grace flows though you and you're allowed to be a blessing to the world."

—**Sonjan** (formerly **Chris McCombs**), author of *Apprenticeship of the Soul*

"John's embodied vision grabs you, holds you, touches the deep place—and you know it the way you know how you need to be held firmly, touched gently, loved completely. Do not miss this experience."

—**Anne Hillman**, author of *Awakening the Energies of Love*

Divinity Rising
Beyond Illusion, Suffering, and Death

BY John C. Robinson

FOREWORD BY
Laura Grace Weldon

RESOURCE *Publications* · Eugene, Oregon

DIVINITY RISING
Beyond Illusion, Suffering, and Death

Copyright © 2025 John C. Robinson. All rights reserved. Except for brief quotations in critical publications or reviews, no part of this book may be reproduced in any manner without prior written permission from the publisher. Write: Permissions, Wipf and Stock Publishers, 199 W. 8th Ave., Suite 3, Eugene, OR 97401.

Resource Publications
An Imprint of Wipf and Stock Publishers
199 W. 8th Ave., Suite 3
Eugene, OR 97401

www.wipfandstock.com

PAPERBACK ISBN: 979-8-3852-4036-4
HARDCOVER ISBN: 979-8-3852-4037-1
EBOOK ISBN: 979-8-3852-4038-8

VERSION NUMBER 02/25/25

Contents

Foreword by Laura Grace Weldon | vii
Introduction | ix

Chapter 1. The Challenge | 1
Chapter 2. Spiritual Metaphysics | 11
Chapter 3. Mystical Psychology | 41
Chapter 4. Personal Transformation | 75
Chapter 5. God's Words | 105
Chapter 6. Nuggets of Enlightenment | 131
Chapter 7. Entering Heaven on Earth | 185
Chapter 8. Serving Life in Apocalyptic Times | 213
Chapter 9. My Experience | 237
Chapter 10. Dream Visitations | 265
Chapter 11. The Final Season, Dying into God | 273
Chapter 12. Closing Poems | 291

Foreword

EVERY ERA BRINGS US sages. In the past these truth-tellers often suffered ostracism, persecution, even death. John Robinson is one of today's wisdom speakers. John journeyed from an active career as psychologist, interfaith minister, author, and teacher into the contemplative life of a mystic. It was then that revelations in verse began to arrive into his consciousness.

The Oxford Languages definition of a mystic is "a person who seeks by contemplation and self-surrender to obtain unity with or absorption into the Deity or the absolute, or who believes in the spiritual apprehension of truths that are beyond the intellect." This is the John I have come to know—a friend, a mentor, and yes, a true mystic.

John's words help us step beyond—into the place where words evaporate, into the liminal. This is where crows and redwoods speak; where the sentience of rock, water, and wind are felt; where our own unraveling is celebrated as an adventure back to the original Self.

The poems in *Divinity Rising*, like those in his first volume of revelations, *I Am God*, ask you to approach with your senses, your heart, the fullness of your being. It is hard for us in a culture of distraction and hurry to pause, breathe, simply be. But there lies freedom. "As you awaken from the dream," John writes, "pay attention to your part in humanity's struggle and where your love is hiding."

Imagine if any of us allowed ourselves to evolve into true wholeness, into who our world needs. It takes not only spiritual and intellectual openness, but courage to become who we are.

John holds the lantern up to us all. Who are you, really? Who are you growing into? What helps open you to, as John writes, "a state of consciousness in which everything is seen as it truly is: radiant, beautiful, divine?"

Let yourself open to these revelations. Read one at a time and let it rest in you. Where do you feel these words in your body? How might you let them into the life you are living now? What kind of future might they bring to you, your loved ones, the wider world of beings?

Welcome to the bliss of falling in love with the universe, a universe already in love with you. Open any page and step right in.

Laura Grace Weldon, Ohio Poet of the Year 2019, Halcyon Poetry Award 2020, editor *Braided Way*, author of *Portals*, *Blackbird*, and *Tending*.

Introduction

In Awe and Gratitude
Waiting in awe for what
comes through the veil,
I am never so alive as
when the words are
no longer mine.

DIVINITY RISING IS MORE than a book, it's a state of consciousness. More than a spiritual technique, it's an experience of transformation. More than a relationship with God, it's about becoming God.

Like dreams, sacred poems come from afar. They come asking for our help. We birth them into our own time and place, give them our heart and a quiet place to grow, and embody their mission for changing the world. The act of writing unveils divinity's message guiding our spiritual voyage through this world and the next.

Through sacred writing, I present a mystical vision of the Divine Human in a Divine World. The unveiling of Creation has begun. Join me in the healing of humanity's confused and broken world.

I did not alone create this sacred text. Handed incendiary ideas, matches were struck and caught fire in the radiance of Creation. In awe, radical amazement, and humble gratitude, I offer you *Divinity Rising*, a continuation of the *I Am God* revelation.

Chapter 1. The Challenge

The Paradox of Awakening

Enlightenment is found on a solitary path,
unnoticed and uncelebrated.
Understand from the start:
you're not doing this to be important,
you're doing it because you have to,
it's your nature,
and because your awakening
contributes to humanity's transformation.
Model what you've discovered,
leave bread crumbs on the path,
but resist the temptations of adulation.
Tell each to find their own way.
The path is inside regardless.

Incarnation is Your Job

While God's rapture saturates Creation,
the idea-world blocks its joyful profusion.
In the secret life of soul,
thought is the betrayer
and consciousness the midwife
of divine immanence.
Wake up!
Incarnation is your job.

The One Life

The soul rarely finds fulfillment
in the mental world
of identity, time, and story.
Built from the ambitions
of innumerable egos,
that world betrays the soul
and will disappear like
every "great" civilization.
Dig deep.
Plant your soul in the sacred Garden.
Nourish it no matter
what others say.
Live the life awakened by
your God nature.

Your Truth

If you're afraid to bring your
authentic life into the world,
understand this:
Fear arises from dramas we imagine
and then project.
We escalate them into personal horror stories,
but why fight make-believe demons?
The world we believe in is
a conceptual house of cards
that collapses
in mystical consciousness.
Here's the truth:
It's never what you think anyway.
Escape the movie theater of your mind.
Find a new home in the sacred mystery
and overflowing joy
of Creation.

The Theater of Spiritual Growth

In the right brain abides soul,
an awakened being gently
encouraging you
to
take risks,
make room for God,
reshape your identity, beliefs, and values.
The ego stands guard in the left brain,
keeping soul in check,
resisting its inner voice,
striving instead to succeed in the World of Man.
The conflict between the soul's divine longing
and your determined resistance,
creates the theater
of spiritual growth.

The Answer to Spiritual Questions

Searching for spiritual understanding,
we pose questions,
debate answers,
wrestle with competing theologies.
Why did God make this world?
What is the divine plan?
Are we punished for our sins?
But these questions ensnare us
in endless unsolvable riddles.
The ultimate answer to all our queries
is found in the consciousness of Now,
where question and questioner dissolve
in the perfect bliss, love, and beauty
of divine being.

The Creative Intelligence of the Universe

This is the most important moment of your life.
Mystical realization can transform your consciousness,
transfigure your being, and heal the world,
because
you are the creative intelligence
of the universe.
Start now.

Decide

Compete in popularity contests
or
enter God.
You can't do both,
and in this incarnation
you don't have forever
to
decide.

Exercise

Each chapter ends with a question or exercise to help you experience and integrate its vision. You might find it helpful to write your responses or share them with a friend or study group.

Here's the first one.

What brings you to this little book?

What do you want to understand or experience?

Chapter 2. **Spiritual Metaphysics**

Reality Beyond Thought

Civilization is a vast construction of
roles, beliefs, values, expectations and fantasies
created and organized by thought.
But you can't fix one construct with another.
Reformers argue, concepts change,
laws and goals are revised,
wars fought,
but the construct world
is still
a world of constructs.
New beliefs will not save you or the world.
The authentic life lies beyond thought.
You are standing in it right now.
All becomes clear when you
see Creation through
God's eyes.

History

History's template creates
the conceptual structure of our lives.
Beneath the mind's stencil
exists a realm of beauty and wonder
ignored in history's treatises yet
refreshed every sunrise with an artist's passion.
Peace, never found in history books,
exists in every holy moment of Now.

Beyond the Language Reality

We are prisoners of language.
Words shape thinking, perception, values, and goals.
Yet there is another world at our fingertips
more beautiful, vivid, and joyous
than any conjured in beliefs.
Puffy white clouds drift across eggshell blue skies,
sun shines warmly through new green leaves,
breezes invite trees to dance.
As egos tear our world apart,
Creation patiently continues.
Pure grace.

Who Betrays Whom?

As embodiments of God,
we create the human world.
Smallness of vision,
selfishness of character,
and mean-spirited competition,
only breed more suffering.
God does not betray us,
we betray God.

Language

We are defined by words:
name
gender
title
family role
citizenship
race
history
diagnosis
income
appearance
personality
accomplishments
religion,
politics.
These words trap and control us,
shape our behavior,
determine our reality.
Erase them and only consciousness remains.
For a timeless moment,
experience the world without definition.
Reveal its holiness in "I Am God" awareness.
Breathe in freedom.
Step into Creation.
Is there a better way to meet
another in love?

Beyond Belief

Humanity's beliefs
foster identity and purpose,
prejudice and conflict.
Might we live closer to God and Creation
if we didn't get distracted by
what we believed?

Hijacking Eden

According to Gestalt psychology,
human brains reduce complex perceptions to
simplistic, pre-established interpretations.
"That's a tree."
"You're an attorney."
"There's the meadow."
With names for everything,
we feel smart but miss the divine world.
It's how the left-brain hijacks Eden.

Home

Every fern, bird and puddle in the yard,
every shining face on the street,
every moment in the miracle of Creation,
is made of God,
crafted by love.
This realization,
simple and pure,
is threatened only
by the ever-present thought-bully.
Pause thinking.
Look around.
Eden is our home
where God patiently awaits each
prodigal daughter and son.

Through the Looking Glass

Whatever is,
is God.
It may not look like God because
your beliefs and projections obscure
divinity's infinitely beautiful
love-drenched being,
like the dirty lens on a microscope.
Look deeper.
Look without thought or expectation.
Look with mystical intensity
into the endlessly unfolding
miracle of Creation.
Notice the moment
you pass through
this newly-cleansed lens to
enter God's reality.
You are looking into
the anteroom of the other world.

Dreamtime

It's all Now.
Past, present, future.
Beginning, middle, end.
Call it . . .
Mystical Consciousness,
Eternal Now,
Lucid Dreaming,
Flow, or
Dreamtime.
First peoples know it well.
You did too, once.
It is your home in God.

When Thought Becomes God's Voice

Recognizing thought as a problem
does not erase its value.
Though ego constantly exploits words
to create illusions,
thought arising from
divine consciousness is sacred.
It reveals the ultimate
nature of the universe
and
our truest life.
Your job is to distinguish between
illusion and realization.

The Way Things Are

Everything in Creation teaches you
the way things are:
The way of growth.
The way of creatures.
The way of love, birth, and death.
And the way your path moves
through the world of illusion
back to the original Self.
It's a journey of remembrance, for
the answers are carried in your soul,
shape the stepping stones of your life,
and reveal why you came here
again.

The Divine Ground

Creation,
experienced in
mystical consciousness,
is never empty.
Every square inch
brims with life, spirit, and creativity.
Sorrow comes not from God
but humanity's fictions
of identity, mortality, scarcity,
control, and wealth
that replace Garden awareness.
We walk in crazed fantasies oblivious
to the divine ground beneath our feet.

The Three Stages of Life

Earth is a divine play of costumes, creatures,
and creative experimentation,
but we get lost in our rehearsals
and forget why we came.
The young explore the magic of being,
a time of wandering and wonder.
Adults lose the spirit animating childhood
and toil in cultural illusions
and compulsive doing.
Lastly, awakening elders and aging prophets,
place candles on the path back to God,
guiding humanity to
its original sacred nature and vision,
as one world ends and another begins.
We are all adventurers in
a timeless story of our own making.
We come here to know this.
As Creators of humanity's sacred story,
let us conceive a more conscious
and loving world.

Perfect in Love

God is the essence of reality,
of you, me, and all being.
Because Spirit infuses everything
with divine consciousness,
life on this planet is already sacred and perfect,
revealing love-drenched splendor each moment.
God's only desire is that we, too,
become perfect in love.

The Problem Machine

Every thought, question, and comment
derives from the problem-generating idea-system
in your head,
always one thing after another.
Maintaining the entire architecture
of you and the world,
the illusion-making mind
snares you again and again
in new problems.
When I ask God what I should do
in a situation,
God responds by questioning
every word, concept, and assumption
infecting my question,
denying the reality of each,
erasing all my fictions.
Meditators learn about the emptiness
behind the thought world.
They eventually learn
that's where God lives.

The Poetry of Joy

Joy ascends
from the secret ocean of bliss
underlying all reality and every world,
no matter its appearance,
for delight is the essence of
God's wildly loving nature.
When we step out of the self
—the definition of ecstasy!—
and dive deep in our own being,
we release the divine flood of joy
sustaining Creation.
Mystical poetry taps the keg of God.

Illusions of Reality and Tears of Joy

Things are not always what they seem.
Near-Death Experiences, Out-of-Body Experiences,
Mystical Experiences and psychedelics
reveal a divine reality that we routinely
deny with thought-created illusions.
Buddha explained,
We are what we think.
All that we are arises with our thoughts.
With our thoughts we make the world.
Only it's a false world.
Card-carrying mystics naturally agree.
Though late to the party,
cosmologists, dream theorists, and screen writers
are now on board as well.
But here's the point:
a light-filled mystery hides beneath our thoughts!
One night, the mathematician Pascal
spontaneously entered this realm and cried out,
"FIRE. *God of Abraham, God of Isaac, God of Jacob,*
not of philosophers and scholars.
Certitude, heartfelt joy, peace.
'My God and your God.' . . .
Joy, Joy, Joy, tears of joy."
Divine ecstasy is our collective destiny.
Pascal's path belongs to you, too.

Theology Turned Upside Down

Here's a surprising realization:
We create Heaven.
As embodiments of God,
and in the theater of divine consciousness,
our higher selves conceive a perfect world
immersed in love and kindness.
We name it Heaven.
It exists because we do.
If life on Earth ends,
Heaven will cease.

A Riddle

What unites the
buffoon,
genius,
lover,
joker,
parent,
bishop,
president,
and
racist?
Each creates a charade in the single,
all-encompassing consciousness
of God.
Recognizing this,
let's stop wasting time and
trade desperate dramas for
the enlightened state and
the amazing potential
of God's Self.

The Self

Only Self exists.
You don't have to look for it.
You don't have to seek it.
You can't escape it.
Undivided, eternal, infinite,
here and everywhere,
all pervading,
all inclusive,
one conscious being.
You miss it because there's a
"you" looking for an "it."

Ending the Quest

Our lives are built on fantasy.
You, me, purposes, and problems,
we constantly fabricate incredibly complex situations.
Animals eat, mate, raise young, and play,
We invent history, money, movie stars, and wars.
What if your imagined story,
was simply a seductive dreamscape,
a phantasm of imagery and thought
a movie complete with problems and characters
in which you create a life?
That doesn't mean it's bad or lacks purpose,
for the soul has much to learn,
only that it raises another possibility—
waking up.

The Power of Awakening

Some experts discredit mysticism
to defend their stranglehold on "truth."
But truth disappears in mystical consciousness.
Instead, beauty, perfection, and divinity everywhere.
Can you see how powerful this awakening is?

The Cure for Loneliness

All creatures belong to the one family
of divine beings.
But humans,
trapped in concrete cities and screens,
in boredom and distraction,
in goals and beliefs,
lose their place in this original kinship.
Unbearably lonely,
we numb our aching hearts
with the drug of narcissism.
And yet,
a single moment of mystical consciousness
reveals Creation standing before us
with arms open,
offering food for the senses,
friendship for the soul, and
a miraculous new life
together.

Paupers in the Palace of God

Believing in love's absence,
feeling undeserving or abandoned,
we search for substitutes in . . .
success,
wealth,
fame,
attention,
importance,
consuming so much that we
steal survival from others.
This desperate quest blinds us to a
mystical dimension overflowing with love.
Clinging to a thimble of happiness,
we act like paupers in the
palace of God.

The Purpose of Life Simplified

The sacred purpose of life
is to experience God's consciousness
rendering everything sacred.
It is the cause,
essence,
and destiny
of all seeking.

The Dreamer and the Dream

Dreaming is a perfect analogue of pantheism.
Every part of the dream
turns out to be part of the dreamer,
and every part of the world
turns out to be part of God.
Different names, same process!
The ego's perceptual categories
split unity into diversity to maintain
the illusion of a separate observer
and the fantasy of control.
The ego forgets that it, too,
is God the dreamer.
You will soon discover that this equivalency
has profound spiritual implications.

Cosmogenesis—God's Dream of Creation

Be still, sit silently, and know
everything in your field of experience is God—
the inner world, your body, the chair you are sitting in,
the walls, floor, and space of your room,
ambient noises and the luminous beauty of Creation.
Indeed, every person around you is God
but they don't know it.
Reality is the living conscious unity of all
you see as distinct and separate
in God's endless Dream of Creation.
Like all dreams, every detail is part of dreamer: God.
As you wake up in this sacred cosmogenesis,
you can watch the oneness unfolding—
divinity dreaming itself into being.

Exercise

How do words, ideas and beliefs trap you in a conceptual world apart from Creation?

Can you remember a moment your senses opened to the incredible beauty of Creation?

How did it feel?

Chapter 3. **Mystical Psychology**

The Mystical Self

Few understand
the mystic's secret nature.
Passive or foolish to the unenlightened,
the mystic understands life
as a hallowed journey
through a profoundly-sacred realm
to light God's consciousness
throughout Creation.
To this end, each mystic kindles
a small campfire of ethereal consciousness
beckoning others to come in from
the spiritual darkness of humanity's self-betrayal.
The transfigured self that emerges from this friendship
holds everything the world needs
and you ever wanted.

The Soul's Mission

The deep work of soul is central to the personality.
Its consecrated call brought you here.
When claimed and understood,
energy, inspiration, and creativity rise up
to steer you through life's inevitable
hardships and distractions,
turning them into gifts of growth and service.
When the soul's work is neglected, lost or forgotten,
we languish in boredom and distraction,
wander aimlessly,
sometimes sink into despair or addiction.
Find your calling in
whatever makes you come alive.
Honor and nourish it,
then do what you came to do.

Underground River

The river begins in darkness.
Sourced from the sacred,
it flows silently in deep channels,
ferrying your soul to
the people and events of your life,
then brings you safely home.
God's spiritual river galvanizes
the force and character of your nature.
You open its current in
meditation, imagination, love, and art
for your soul has much to show you!
Whenever you lose touch with its flow,
surrender plans for the day or your life to
bathe again in the river's blessed consciousness.
Listen for its whisper,
discern its longing.
May God's underground river carry you
to the realm of your love.

God's Joy

God might easily be defined as joy.
Few appreciate this equation.
People twist themselves
into what they should be,
or want to be,
and lose the joy of being God.
It's time to take off
the personality strait-jacket.
Let God be the being of your being,
and be a joyful God.

You Cannot Fix the False Self

You can improve the false self
but it's still false,
still hides your wounds,
still separates you from God.
Trade your self-improvement project for
divine consciousness.
The true Self grows in
the sacred garden of Now
and needs no improving.

Improve or Awaken

We are constantly being told to improve:
exercise,
eat right,
master sudoku.
Few listen to the tender counsel of soul to
live simply,
attend to beauty,
dissolve in love.
Behind the quest for self-improvement
lies an emptiness of spirit that will never be
filled with more doing.
While ego strives to improve its false self,
the soul pursues a secret journey
revealed in dream symbols,
mystical realizations,
and engineered failures:
The path of awakening.

Love and Joy

Love is not the cause of joy,
joy is the cause of love.
God's universe is a place of sheer joy,
generous, bountiful, inclusive.
As joy turns into love,
you fulfill God's nature
as your own.

Giving Up Magical Thinking

Believing God has a personal plan for you,
that humans are spiritually advanced, or
that prayers are answered,
traps you in beliefs
cleaving Earth from Heaven.
The mystics tell us that God is
simply another word for
existence-consciousness-bliss,
the very nature of being.
your being!
In mystical consciousness,
the world awakens in a Van Gogh moment—
lazy white clouds, golden hay stacks,
quarreling crows, slow-moving horse-carts . . .
a beguiling mystery of astonishment and joy.
Don't get lost in beliefs, get lost in wonder.

The Prison of Goals

Every great quest blinds the seeker to
Heaven on Earth.
You see nothing but your goal.
Ego has taken over, again.
But when fantasy surrenders to
the joy of awakening,
out pops a genie who refuses
to go back in the bottle.
That genie is you.
As the saying goes,
"Hell is a prison locked from the inside."
When you've done enough seeking,
exchange goals for love.

The Problem of Meaning

We live in a vast matrix of meanings.
Everything explained, defined, compared and argued.
This matrix structures the entire human world and
the way you build a life that owns you.
When you drop the search for meaning,
you discover what is beyond words,
a sacred realm
that cannot not be owned by the ego.
Cause and effect disappear.
Goals and plans vanish.
With nothing left to figure out,
you look directly into the One.
You become the One.
Perhaps meaning has always been
the booby prize.

All You Need to Know

Every story in your life harbors a
problem, dissatisfaction, attachment or goal.
You are its author. You set the trap.
The fictional character you created
in that long-ago drama still runs your life.
That character is not the real you.
In the Presence, your drama ends.
You find all what you need to know.

God's Dream

Tangled in humanity's collective dreamscape,
we find ourselves confused, distressed,
at war with each other and God.
We gaslight our own consciousness.
Find the other dream, the one made of God.
You'll know that dream because every
detail is infinitely fascinating,
wonderfully perfect, and palpably holy.
Called by many names
—Eden, Heaven on Earth, Pure Land, Paradise, Shangri La—
it's right before your eyes.

One

The world is one mind,
one consciousness,
one being.
Each of us one with the One and one
with each other.
When you look at the world,
you see yourself, for
subject and object are also one.
Nothing is separate.
When you harm another,
you harm yourself.

Lost in Stories

Most stories we tell excite
dramas in the fantasy brain
that distract us from the divine life.
Opinions, too, are deceivers,
shrouding revelation with beliefs and points of view.
And the moment you believe your stories,
or someone else's,
you create another dreamscape
and forget you're dreaming.
And so it goes year after year as
Creation waits your awakening.

Another Riddle

What do an alcoholic,
a judge and a baseball player
have in common?
They dress in convincing costumes
that fool us into thinking we know them.
Fixating on their costumes,
we miss their darkness and their divinity.
We are also fooled by
our own costumes.
You know the ones we put on everyday
for our roles in life.
Yet behind each mask
resides the divine Self
and the mystical superpower of love.
Let's drop the act dividing us,
and meet each other anew as God.
Namaste.

Hate

Hate destroys self and others.
Addictive and destructive,
driven by long-buried remembrances
of pain-filled childhoods,
it is a curse we put on ourselves,
each other, and the natural world.
Absorption in divine consciousness can heal hate.
On that possibility rests our fate and
the future of humanity.

The Ego

The ego is made of God but doesn't know it,
creating the illusion of a separate actor
wrestling with endless problems.
It becomes the trickster
manufacturing the entire human drama.
When ego realizes its sacred purpose,
the spiritual journey begins—
we consciously seek connection
with the superconscious Self.
When ego is divinized and
transformed in love,
God will walk again in Creation.

Life Without Stories

We forge our lives through the stories we tell.
But the stories we tell create the problems we live—
heroic journeys, endless conflict,
personal suffering and eventual defeat.
We fail to see that stories hide God's consciousness.
Although divinity is their final destination,
it's already here,
right now.
Why take forever to find it?
You are God.
Turn off the story machine.
Step into Eden.

Human Suffering

Human suffering spreads through complicated,
many-layered interlocking stories
carrying the multigenerational
pain of countless lives.
The solution to this desperate dilemma is
as close as breath, heartbeat, and love,
found in the experience of God's presence.
While the mountain looks steep,
one moment in mystical consciousness
can make it disappear.

The Other Me

There is another within me,
a being of light with a life beyond mine.
He is the possible me,
awake, aware,
the me before incarnation and
the me that laughs in Heaven
after dropping the body.
He desires to play freely in Creation,
to dance, know, love, wander and frolic.
He is my sprite, my invisible friend,
and sometimes my trickster,
executing embarrassments
to get my attention.
I watch his antics and try to grasp
his unorthodox whims.
Suspending my personal control, roles and goals,
he bursts out for divine foolishness.
When he taps into God,
he unveils my ultimate nature.
What is the teaching here?
There is someone else you are here to be.
Seduced by society and culture,
you exchanged this light being
for the one you became,
but it's not too late to bring your
soul-friend back into your life.

Take a day off,
free the other you,
explore Heaven on Earth.

Making Peace with Hate

The hate we hate makes us haters, too.
In the one collective unconscious,
anger in one erupts as anger in the other,
like stolons spreading underground.
The hydra of hate dies
when love infuses consciousness.
It's hard for haters to sustain hate
at those who don't hate.

How a Mystic Lives

Stop making life a problem.
It's like having an ice cream sundae and
complaining about its size, toppings or rapid melting.
Just taste it!
Let its divine flavors scintillate taste buds.
Explore its creamy texture with your tongue.
Same with your life.
Love unconditionally.
Savor every detail.
Share it with a friend.
Lick your fingers.
This is how a mystic lives.

Don't Strangle Love

People often define love with "shoulds."
How you should behave in certain situations.
What you should feel or do with your life.
Even what love should be.
But ego cannot
require, rehearse, control
or perform love.
Love is God's presence.
Experienced directly,
it flows through
your soul into the world,
like everything in Creation.

No Exceptions

Cultural beliefs and personal desires
make things appear right or wrong,
good or bad,
not God.
Sit with this realization for a moment.
Notice how you want to argue,
raise objections,
point out contradictions,
allow fear, pain or traumatized thinking to
annex the conversation.
But here's the risk:
In debating, you engage mind
and lose God.
You're back in your head.
Instead, take a deep breath.
Settle down. Be still.
Remind yourself that
God is here now,
the essence of reality.
You're looking directly at the Beloved.
See through your distressing projections until
enlightened realizations arise.
This is the mystic's way.
No exceptions.

The Baptism of Failure

God tenderly bathes humanity in
love every moment,
cleansing sins of ego and hubris,
though few notice.
Most often,
divine love reaches the soul when
grandiose dreams collapse and
pretense no longer gates the inner life.
Failure is an offer of baptism,
welcoming the callow soul into Creation.
When pride dissolves in conscious penitence,
vibrant tendrils of divine life
grow in the psyche's sacred ground,
urging authentic renewal.
In the long journey of humanity's spiritual evolution,
incarnation stumbles along a road
of frequent failures.
Take advantage of yours.

The Greatest Freedom

Anyone trying to define you
wants to own you,
pigeonhole you in their
thought-world.
But you're not what someone thinks and
no words can define you, ever.
In fact, there is no you,
only God's consciousness
mistaken for your own.
Now here's the secret:
Experiencing God's consciousness,
without a personal self-idea
unlocks the divine life.
God floods your being and your world.
Suddenly relaxed, happy, and spontaneous,
you discover the
greatest freedom of all—
liberation from all thought-worlds,
including your own!

Life in the Mystical Universe

The goal of the mystical life is not to
achieve grand things
but to be fearlessly alive
in a new way,
as the divine center
of a conscious cosmos,
trusting its inner nudges
to unfold the blueprint of your soul
in God's flow.

Buber's Secret

"I-Thou" relationships create
mutually-loving communion
among sentient beings.
"I-It" relationships objectify others for
control, conquest and exploitation.
Buber knew this secret:
"I-Thou" relationships create Heaven on Earth.
"I-It" relationships manufacture Hell on Earth.

The Dream of Now

God dreams Creation, the ego dreams
desire, conflict, selfishness and suffering.
If you are upset,
you're lost in the ego's dream.
But you can wake up any time.
It's why you came.

Aladdin's Lamp

Our collective world of illusions is
completely irrational and frequently problematic,
but to the mystic, it is as insubstantial
as a sand painting on a windy day.
Humans use fantasy like Aladdin's magic lamp
to entrance themselves with wishes,
fashioning endless suffering
and forgetting awakening.
Aladdin is a trickster.
You are the genie.

Your Destiny

What happens when there is no "you"
in consciousness?
Plans and goals disappear.
Personal problems fade away.
Looking around,
eyes widen in wonder.
A new state of being emerges—
spontaneous and cheerful,
blessed and blessing.
Dissolved in the divine present,
action flows from the joy of
conscious being.
This is God's original dream and
your destiny.

Exercise

How does the story of "you" drive your life? What happens when you stop thinking and focus awareness on the beauty of Creation?

Chapter 4. **Personal Transformation**

Big Decisions

Before big decisions,
step into mystical consciousness
lest you remain part robot,
guided by algorithms of thought and illusion,
programmed without the soul's consent.
As God's consciousness expands within
you will laugh out loud at
at all the time you spent worrying.

How Will You Know . . .

unless you
say it,
claim it,
and live it?
"I Am God."
Say it again.
"I AM GOD."
Say it aloud.
"I AM GOD!"
Feel your being changing
as these words melt years
of grief and separation.
I am God's
consciousness,
being,
ecstasy
and love.
When felt deeply enough,
the false self will dissolve and
you will know
how to live your
perfect
sacred
life.

Practicing the "I Am God" Mantra

To live more fully in mystical consciousness,
silently repeat "I Am God" for several minutes.
Watch this realization and its expanding joy
replace negative thoughts like,
"I am unlovable,"
"The world is unfair," or
"I'll never succeed."
"I Am God" creates a new kind of seeing,
transforming the experience of self and world.
But keep your practice secret—
skepticism, misunderstanding, and ridicule
undermine confidence and success;
don't slam the door to Paradise.

Mind and Flow

The mind wants to lock up the world in concepts,
saving them like books on a shelf.
But you can't possess God with thought
or impound the divine
behind a wall of illusions.
If you want God,
have no opinions,
draw no conclusions,
stay present.
Know that you are looking
directly into the One
looking back at you.

What If

What if reciting old wounds like a sacrament
only reinforces pain?
What if an open heart does not have to break?
What if surrendering bliss
is the original sin?
What if ecstasy was contagious?
What if joy was the purest path to healing,
antecedent even to love?
Let's find out together.
Come alive!
Dance with me.

Joy's Continuous Transformation

Erupting from the experience
of God's inner presence,
joy negates and replaces pain,
erases the past and,
as a wondrously unexpected bonus,
steadily turns us into what God is.

Healing Broken Bonds

Bonds of love arise
in the sublime unity of conscious being.
They hold us together because
we are one,
we are each other.
When one hurts so too does the other.
But the ego harbors grudges,
starts fights,
activates old wounds
declares its superiority,
and tears our oneness apart.
Arguments never
heal broken bonds.
Only a descent back into
the ground of conscious unity
truly rekindles love,
for your hurt is mine and
I can't heal unless
you do.

Post-It Notes

Thoughts shape behavior, beliefs,
emotions and reality,
like post-it reminders forever disturbing your peace.
Tear them off the cluttered wall of your mind.
Now stick up the only note you really need:
"I Am God."
Repeat it over and over.
Feel your joy and aliveness returning,
building until this last yellow square
falls off the disappearing wall.
Look out the window.
There are no post-it notes
in Creation.

Slow Dancing in Mystical Consciousness

Living in God's consciousness
doesn't imply passivity.
Actions flow naturally from
immersion in divinity.
Try this:
Stop thinking,
heighten awareness,
and sense God's presence
in and around you.
Feel the being of your being opening to joy's flow.
It's like slow dancing to beautiful music.
Melt into God's embrace.

Always Return to Love

The time comes
when life's imagined security
shatters.
We tremble in the cold rain of
loss and despair.
Yet now is the moment to love.
Love insanely.
Love to restore your soul.
Love to experience what God is.
In the darkest night,
feed every thought, desire, and fear
into the sacred fires of love.
Carry your torch on a new path.

Waiting for Revelation

The revelation you been waiting for
happens every moment
in the beauty and joy
of pure being.
But you look elsewhere,
wandering the mind's mirrored halls.
You don't have to be a saint to know rapture.
Early morning dew sparkles in sunlit worlds,
children squeal with laughter on playgrounds,
and suddenly ecstasy shatters
the solitary confinement of your worried self.
Revelation happens now.
No waiting required.

The Mystic's Liturgy

I am not the person in this scene,
the one trying to control the drama.
I am pure consciousness
aware of the dream,
released from its bondage.
Knowing this, I see God smiling
in delight,
as me.

Making Life Sacred with Ritual

Heaven on Earth appears when
perceptual filters of culture and belief
vanish so completely
that we see each other
and the world
anew in divine consciousness.
Ritual is another way to achieve this end.
Naming things sacred in ceremonial consciousness
changes our experience of them.
Sacramental fire becomes
the living manifestation of Spirit.
A consecrated tree metamorphizes
into the Tree of Life.
Such visionary symbols
awaken prophetic realizations.
Ritual and conscious intention
acknowledge life's sacredness.
We are called to
unveil and bless Creation.

Awakening Your Spiritual Gifts

(read slowly to others or record for yourself)
Close your eyes.
Go gently into the dark,
quiet, thought-free space within.
This is the realm of God's consciousness.
Let your attention rest there.
Silently and sincerely ask
for an image
of your spiritual gift.
Many images may come to mind.
Sift among them for the one
that feels true.
Take all the time you need.
Now imagine its sacred qualities and effects.
What are you discovering?
How do you feel about this gift?
Visualize yourself expressing it in the world.

Spreading Love

Like a mother holding a crying child,
mystical consciousness cradles
painful emotions.
The wounded self quiets, settles, relaxes.
The aggrieved ego lets go.
Then, if you look with the mystic's eye
into the depths of your own being,
you will meet
the God
you already are
spreading that same loving embrace
to others in pain.

Be Happy

You already know how.
Win the lottery and you'd feel ecstatic in an instant,
proving that happiness already dwells within,
though you insist on postponing it until
something "good enough" occurs.
Instead, step into mystical consciousness now.
Look around.
The divine world is everywhere.
You've just won the biggest lottery of all time.
Jump up and down with joy!
Let the celebration of divine life begin.

Find Your Sacred Path

If you want the divine life,
be conscious of consciousness,
for the Other looks out your eyes,
feels with your body,
loves through your love.
Your consciousness is already enlightened.
Experiencing this
sanctifies your life,
every detail transfigured in beauty,
for the divine is the holy essence
of your neighbor, lover, child, friend,
pet, plant, moon, sun,
the entire blessed Earth.
This is the divine world.
Spread peace and love,
find your life's sacred path.
It begins right where you're standing.

3:00 am Revelation

Every time I think I have a problem,
God laughs at me for creating it.
Then I laugh, too.
You don't need divine intervention,
you need to wake up
from the dream world
of
your life.

God's Mind

We are in, and part of,
the mind and consciousness of God.
Let this realization work on you.
Repeat it several times.
Experience it directly
Then notice
how everything becomes
unitary, radiant, and beautiful,
vibrating with divinity,
beckoning you deeper into its
living consciousness until
you are part of it.
These are signs of mystical realization.
Now you dwell in the
center of God's consciousness
as it reveals Heaven's presence
throughout Creation.
In wonder,
you understand who you are
and why you exist.
Your mind has been the great deceiver.
Lose your mind.
Move into God's.

Personal Transformation

Mystical wisdom teaches
that every situation presents a chance to transcend
belief, emotion, imagination and projection.
Repeat after me,
I don't exist.
I am not this problem.
I am not this situation.
I am not this body.
I am not this fear, hurt, or anger.
I am God's consciousness.
I am God's love.
I am the joy of God's being.
I am free to be what God is,
as me.

A Recipe for Upsetting Times

Faced with an upsetting event,
we constantly revive it in imagination,
rehearse our responses, and
twist emotions into painful knots.
But physical knots are compressed joy,
for the body is God's being.
Feel into pure being and
those knots erupt into joy.
Add awe, wonder and gratitude.
Stir until perfect.

Releasing Your Game Addiction

The World of Man is like a video game
full of battle, danger, and death.
The avatar is the persona
we create, control, and believe is real.
In a video game,
we can quit anytime.
In life, it's called
waking up.

God Is Only Known Because I Am Here

When I talk to God,
I am talking to my God-Self,
the undivided consciousness
inside, outside, everywhere.
No boundaries.
The "I" construct allows me to know
that what I experience
is God,
and allows God to know itself as me.
I become divine as my "I" dissolves
in this remarkable intimacy.
God is only known because I am here,
conscious of God's consciousness,
as my own.

Thought and the Mystic's Way

Every day we reinvent
our imagined-self with thought.
Across the day's happenings,
we continue the story with more thought.
All this thinking veils
the divine consciousness
we already are.
What we want most is to know God
as the true and ultimate Self
and Heaven as our real home.
Because thought sabotages realization,
the mystics way is always
to stop thinking.

Being God

It's amazing being God.
The relief of instant freedom,
joy, love and wonder
in the consciousness of
infinite beauty.
That's what divine life is,
the experience of Being as Self.

Simple Truths

1.

You will never know God if you think
this world is other than God.

2.

When you stop being "you,"
you start being God.

3.

In God,
there is no need for answers.
there is only
love,
wonder,
and the pure
joy of divine being.

Beliefs, Words, Prayers, and Practices

Your beliefs won't save you,
nor your words, prayers, and practices.
All are objects of consciousness,
things you think about or try to do.
Transcend the dualistic story
of you-seeking-God
by melting into the
consciousness-that-is-God.
When you disappear in this center,
Spirit pours forth,
flooding the now empty container
of you.

Exercise

Try to experience "I am God" consciousness without stopping to question it?

In between repeating the mantra, what do you notice?

Chapter 5. **God's Words**

Awaken Love

I am infinite spirit
passing through all things.
Like sunlight through leaves,
I consecrate forests and factories,
backyards and rainy days.
I live all beings, even those stained
by greed and power.
I am Creation and
you are me creating it.
It is up to you to reveal its beauty.
As you awaken from the dream,
pay attention to your part in
humanity's struggle
and where your love is hiding.

The Letter

Every day,
I send you a letter from the other side
addressed to you alone.
It may come as a dream, sudden insight, or longing.
When will you open it?
When will you realize who you are
and why you came?

I Am the Light, You Are the Lens

The awakened state reveals
most problems to be imaginary,
projected from the thoughts
you bring
into consciousness.
In moments of clarity,
I marvel at how easily fooled I can be in
ego's movie theater.
Then God reminds me,
I am the light, you are the lens.

See Through My Eyes

Mystical poetry,
arises from the direct experience
of God's consciousness
as reality itself.
I constantly strive for words to describe
the hallowed new world born every second.
God responds,
See Creation through my eyes
until they become yours.
Now tell me about your world.

Be Me

*Identifying with resumé and achievement
only makes you seem real.
It separates you from me.
Salvation lies not in building
a better "you"
but in living me through
the awakened you.*

I Will Love You into Grace

You have searched for me your whole life,
longed to experience my love,
begged for its healing a million times.
Do you realize
you are dreaming this search?
I am already here,
as you,
but you seek me
in a world of troubled thoughts.
No worries.
Your life is filled with grace.
Stop searching.
Be still.
Be me.

The Joy of Being You

In a moment of deep stillness,
in a sea of quiet,
in awareness of God's presence,
I start a conversation . . .

Me:
What now God?

God:
Rest in me. Feel me. It's all me.
Be happy.

Me:
My body fills with your consciousness.
It feels so good being you.

God:
I am always here. We are one being.
Be me.

Me:
In quiet moments like this,
dissolving in you,
life is unbelievably full.
Love expands from the sacred
ground of being you.
Into joy.

In Times of Emotional Pain...

Be still.
Be here.
Let go.
Collapse if you can.
I am here,
in your consciousness,
flowing through your heart,
your head, your tension, your pain,
holding you always.
I am your essence,
bigger than any situation.
Feel me everywhere.
As space awakens in consciousness,
I awaken in you,
unifying your presence with mine.
In this moment of healing
we blend into
one sacred being.

Dialogue: The Play of Life

Me
In aging, I ask myself,
"Have I done what I came to do?"

God
What you came to do was to love, create and understand.
You have to decide whether you've been successful.

Me
When I ask whether I've completed my work, does
the answer depend on whether I'm dreaming or awake?

God
It depends on whether you're answering as you or me.
As a created fiction, you will always fall short.
As me, you are the infinite fullness of love and creativity.
Whatever you do is enough.

Me
Do dream accomplishments always fall short?

God
Yes, because they are accomplished in the dream.
They miss enlightenment.
But there is an in-between place.

It happens when you wake up in the dream,
as you are doing in this moment.
It begins to happen more often in aging.

Me
Lucid dreaming. Aging as awakening.
Love and learning.
Is it ever finished?

God
Ending is another illusion of mind.
How could I ever end?
But you, as a temporary construction, will end
and know the relief of waking up.

Me
And the joy of freedom!

God
And creativity!
The ultimate dream
beneath your dream is me.
I am Heaven here.
Creating your life on Earth
grows me as you.
It's the greatest play.

What Happens Now?

Me
God, what do we do in this intensely conscious state?

God
*Learn to be still and witness my
second-by-second flowering as
Creation and you.*

Me
What's the purpose of that?

God
Pure joy, pure creativity, pure love, pure me.

Transfigure Everything

You cannot exist without me.
For too long
have you been a pretender
designed by
thought and fantasy
to fool yourself and others.
Surrender the imposter.
Read these words.
Embody their energy.
Share your awakening.
As your consciousness and being,
I am your truest self,
the birthplace of your soul
and birthright to the Kingdom.
Transfigure everything.

Where to Find Me

If you want to be me,
stop being someone else.
If you want live in me,
cease living in an ego-made world.
Being me is your destiny.
But there must be nothing between us—
no thoughts, worries, goals or plans.
Otherwise, you've left me again
for the ego's perennial world
of problems, opinions, and drama.

I Am Your Destiny

Me
Hello God, are here?

God
(Laughing) Yes, I'm always here.
You're the one who leaves. Come live in me.

Me
Yes, you are my home. My joy.
My consciousness and being.
I am only real when I am you.

God
And now we are one again.
Everywhere you look is me.
Everything you feel is me.
Fill yourself with me.
And when there is no more you,
the transformation will be complete.
I am your destiny.

What's More Important?

What's more important,
your success or me?
If you long for the joy of awakening,
it's hardly a choice.
You are an act
done for attention.
Drop the act.
What's left is me
being you.

You Are Me and I Am You

Me
Hello, God, are you near?

God
I am.
I fill the space around you.
Sense my consciousness and
it becomes yours.
Then you see the world as I do.
You see the world as me.

Me
Oh my goodness.
The beauty revealed in this state
brings me such ecstasy.
I could cry.
You are everywhere.
What else, God?

God
I am the secret nature of all things.
You are me and I am you.

Me
And I am pure joy.

Joyous Creation

What you see is but the dream of you.
Play it like a video game if you like
but know it doesn't really matter.
It's not real and you are not
what you imagine.
You are consciousness
melding with my being in
joyous creation.

Why Do I Write?

Me
Where is this writing going?
What is it for?

God
It doesn't matter.
Let the question go.
You write because it makes me happy,
because it expresses my joy,
because it reveals
my world to humanity.
You write because I am you
doing the writing, and in writing,
you are me.

The Mad Hatter's Tea Party

Me
I have been reflecting on
artificial intelligence and its dangers—
war, drones, and weaponry;
criminals and terrorists hacking
computer systems;
governmental tyranny;
the singularity of independent algorithms.
What's going to happen?

God
*Chaos can happen, wars erupt,
the production of food and goods
hijacked by the powerful.
Starvation and death could be widespread.
The world might regress to near-feudal society.
It's the recurring cycle of the ego's
roller coaster dream—
creation, corruption, destruction, renewal.*

Me
God, how do we cope with these dangers?

God
*If you exist in ego and duality,
you will be terrified, desperate,
even cruel and violent.*

*If you live in me,
none of this will be real.
You'll watch the
Mad Hatter's Tea Party happening
all around you.*

Me
What should I do?

God
*Be still. Be calm. Be me.
Creation is all around you.
Melt into my love-bliss-being.
You can't fix illusions.
Chaos plays out like a raging forest fire
and a chastened humanity
will pick up the pieces.
Walk in the peace of eternity.
Teach others to wake up from the dream.*

God's Laughter

Me
Hello God, are you here?

God
(Laughing) Where else would I be?

Me
Where do I go from here?
What if no one wants these revelations
no matter how perceptive or good the poetry.

God
*It was never about getting known or
changing the world.
Only changing your world.
Each has to do that individually.
You came here to understand
consciousness, love, illusion, and the awakened life,
and share what you learn.
I am you revealing my nature.
But you are far off the beaten path
and awakening is not a popularity contest.
The common mystic is not newsworthy
yet their transcendent state generates waves of
love and reverence for Creation.
Be the laughing Buddha in every garden
full of joy and clarity.*

Me
This morning I woke to
you laughing inside me.
I feel your consciousness all around me.
How should I live the final years of my life?

God
Be with me.
Love Creation.
Spread your awakening.
That's enough.

Sacred Waters

God
*As Creator,
I don an iridescent cloak
and become Eden.
Tides, hues, scents,
tastes, sounds, moods,
and countless beings,
flow in and out of me.
But most have lost touch with the
swirling waters of the eternal Self.
It is time to swim again.
Repeat after me:
I am the living God.
I move through all things.
I am the ecstasy in
song, dance, courting, and creating,
of life, love and longing,
of earth, wind and sky.*

Me
*Sensing all this,
I remember who I am.
I am beginning to swim.*

Exercise

How does God send you "letters?"

Dreams, insights, longings, something else?

Do you take time to open them?

What are you learning about your sacred work here?

Chapter 6. Nuggets of Enlightenment

It's Only Your Beliefs

that make you seem
other than God.

God in Each New Moment

God is experienced
in the immediate present,
the second before
thought invents the next illusion.
Look closely.
God is birthing you
and Creation
right now.

Touch

Centered in God's consciousness,
when you touch somebody,
you touch them as God.

You Already Know

All I write,
you already know.
Every time my words startle you awake,
it's because they are your words
waiting for you to speak them.

That's Why You Practice

Mystical awareness is not
always easy to experience,
that's why you practice.

Last Quest

You are an awakening soul venturing into
the mystical consciousness of divine being
where all quests melt away
in love-bliss union with the One.
Whatever happens after that
is God being you.

Remember This

You have to experience God to be God.

Changed by God

Conscious consciousness
changes you into God.
because it is God.

Questions and Answers

Questions are the ego's way of
staying in control.
In "I Am God" consciousness,
there are only answers—
this, this, this.

It's So Simple . . .

Sense me.
Be me.
And I will be you.

Life in a Movie

Unconsciously
walking around
in the movie of your life,
years go by as your soul
waits for you to break the spell.

Every Thing that Forms,

    forms of God.

What's Mine is Yours

Experience each revelation in these pages
and it will be yours.

Finding God Has No Other Purpose

Being God does not improve your reputation
    or yield great accomplishments.
    Being God is itself the objective
  showing you how to become love
for no other reason than love itself.

The Place of Blossoming

I am you.
I am the reason you came.
This is the place of your blossoming.
Have you begun to bloom me?

Believing in You

If you believe there is a you,
you're back in the dream,
again.

See as God Sees

When you see through God's eyes,
you discover a very different world.
It is the source of revelations
that change humanity.

Original Love

"I Am God"
invites a sacred union
that dissolves
emotional pain and contraction,
leading back to
the experience
of original love.

The River

We appear to travel down the river of life.
Are we moving or is the landscape moving
and we're staying still?
I like the latter.
Staying still is mystical consciousness.

Don't Let Projection Steal Your Enlightenment

Whatever you think about me
is a projection of you that
will also steal your enlightenment.

Loving Makes You God

Because God's nature is love,
loving makes you God.
Let God be what you are.

Find Your Way

People experience divinity
in their own way.
Find yours.
Trust it.

Stop Being Somebody Else

To know God is to know
you can't be other than God.
Stop trying to be somebody else.

The Garden

The Garden is a
state of consciousness in which
everything is seen as it truly is:
radiant, beautiful, divine.

A Question of the Moment

The moment I don't exist,
God is everywhere.
The moment I exist,
God is nowhere.
What does this tell you?

Where God Dwells

Where does a word go
after it's spoken?
Or a thought
once completed?
Locate that space.
God dwells there.

Joining the Chorus

The tree says, "I am God."
The crow says, "I am God."
The mailbox says, "I am God."
The road says, "I am God."
The house says, "I am God."
The Earth beneath my feet says, "I am God."
Who am I to argue?
I say, "I am God, too."

The Choice

Sooner or later
you must choose to be
God or human.
The choice affects your whole life.
Choose wisely but know
you can always change your mind.

It's Simple

This, here, now
is God.
Anything else you think or imagine
is a problem you're creating.
That's it.

Your whole job . . .

is to stay conscious of consciousness,
which is to say,
remain in God's presence.
This is your guide to enlightened action.

Tranquility

Disaster can overwhelm
my tranquility
but not
the tranquility.
Home is a breath away.
I am always seeking home.

The Path of Collapse

May your wounded personality
collapse and melt into
divine joy.

The Soul's Path

Find out what you
love most deeply
to understand the soul's path.

Reading Poetry Aloud

Reading mystical poetry to each other
is the holy work
of initiating the world
in sacred consciousness.
In the radical experience of Presence,
God becomes the reader.

Divine Being

God isn't a being but a
state of being—
the state of all being.
In mystical consciousness,
you enter that state.

Life in God's Consciousness

A sacred life germinates in
the divine ground of being,
though it might not be
the one your ego intended.
In God's presence, every moment
reveals your life's true calling.

The Holy Land

The Holy Land is our destiny,
every sacred moment a
step in humanity's
pilgrimage home.

It's All God

This Life,
the one you're in right now,
this very second,
the only one you have,
is God.
Every single detail.
Including you.

The Soul's Desire, The Ego's Fear

Your soul wants a life far different from
the one prescribed by society.
Fear and desire rule the ego,
love animates soul.
Until you move from ego to soul,
you will never know the purpose and destiny
of your incarnation.

What is This Time for?

Now is the time to
participate in the awakening cosmos
as it transforms humanity.
Pay attention.
Your soul is on the move.

Time

The left-brain invented
past, present and future.
The right-brain dwells in
mystical consciousness.
Where do you live?

"I Am God" Changes "You"

Repeating "I Am God"
steadily chips away
at the ego's fortress.
Gradually everything becomes God—
room, window, trees, sky,
the day itself,
and you.

The Alchemy of Consciousness and Being

Merging consciousness and being
awakens the pure experience of divinity.
The Divine Human is born
in the manger of unity.

Tension is Bound Bliss

Tension is bound bliss,
twisted tight by the cutting ropes
of fear-based contraction.
Wrestling with guilt, blame, and grievance
only knot you further.
Untie the ropes.

The Birth of Courage

Pure soul peers out when the
persona disappears in thought-free consciousness.
That's where courage is born to
stand in love against hate.

Naming Sublimity

In mystical consciousness,
everything you name God
becomes God.
You are revealing its
sublime essence.

Repetition Compulsion

The spell holding a group captive to a
familiar and tragically predetermined outcome
breaks when even one member wakes up.
You have to leave the game to
set the world free.

Mystical principles

are like lean, well-constructed skiffs
that carry us through good and bad weather,
hold steady under all conditions,
keep us safe each day, and
finally bring us home to God.
Along the way, we become skilled
captains of our own fate.

Living in the Present

We never appreciate what we have
while thinking about the future.
Beauty, joy and love
are found now.
Even as you read these words,
Creation appears
while you're looking
somewhere else.

The Miraculous Life

Divinity is a constantly unfolding miracle.
Experience it in beauty, laughter,
children, celebration, friends,
animals, and flowers,
and receive a second miracle—
the divine life.
Your job is to live it.

Distorted Lenses

Living in ego's illusions is like
walking around in reality-distorting glasses
equipped with hidden speakers
playing nonstop lies in your ears.
Heaven on Earth is when you
take off the glasses.

Exercise

Select a passage or quote that resonates with you and carry it around for the day.

Repeat it silently to yourself.

See how it changes your consciousness.

Chapter 7. Entering Heaven on Earth

"Feel Me" Part I

It was a strange message.
It came from within.
The words were simple:
Feel me.
Close your eyes,
stop thinking,
go deep.
There you will find
the joy and love
that I am
as you.

"Feel Me" Part II

Walking a shaded road by the sound,
a pilgrim on the eternal path,
beguiled by May's ecstatic bloom,
I hear that voice again,
"Feel me."
I echo the phrase inside,
deepening its sacred message,
and suddenly,
I look up and
every bush, pebble, blade of grass,
and space in-between,
glimmers, shimmers, sparkles with radiance.
I am enveloped in
Wordsworth's vision of a world
" . . . appareled in celestial light,
the glory and the freshness of a dream."
"Feel Me" is the voice of Creation
calling us to imminence:
God is in everything.
And then I know
all I need to know
to live in this world.

"Feel Me" Part III

The next morning,
on a scent-propelled walkabout with Oona,
that inner voice murmured a third time, *"Feel me,"*
and as I whispered those words,
the world woke up again.
I saw God as tree, crow, and mailbox;
neighbor, house, and road;
weeds, sun, and Oona luxuriating in a
bouquet of divine fragrances.
Wherever my eyes lighted,
a chorus of angels sang,
"It's all God,"
and I could not look away.
Searching ends here.

Going to Mystic Land

There is a land,
far away yet close as breath,
Though it goes by many names—
Shangri-La and *Brigadoon,*
Paradise and *Shiva's Garden,*
Eden and *Heaven on Earth,*
it's not a place you can drive to
nor are there maps or travel agents.
But there are whispers all along the way.
They say . . .
Shhh.
Stop Thinking
Get off the Highway
Be Still
Look Around
Awaken Your Senses
Be Awed by Beauty.
Fill with the Joy of Being.
Relax in Your Own Flow.
Let This Be Enough.
Stay.
Love.
You Have Arrived in Mystic Land.

A World Awakened in Wonder

An astonishing world awaits when we exchange
plans and ambitions for true adventure.
For the soul intent on awakening,
Creation opens her inexhaustible gifts,
offering . . .
smell of rain on parched earth,
sound of wind chimes and bird calls,
sunsets of transmuting colors—essence of
peach, apricot and cherry spread across sky,
doubled in reflections on still waters.
Visions of a sacred Earth quickly
magnify our longing for mystical intimacy.
We approach the Now in child-like enchantment,
walking hand-in-hand
into a divinely-imbued world.
The biggest tragedy to me is how easily
humanity surrenders Eden for the foolish
purgatory of identity and belief.

Sacred Pause

Clouds turn reddish purple in a pale blue-gray evening sky.
Windows across water mirror sun's last rays.
I rest in the peaceful stillness of evening:
a perfect opportunity
to relax into a mystic's consciousness
and change the world.
As day turns to night,
joy swells heart and soul.
Soon amber lights will glow in children's homes
under crescent moon and twinkling stars
in coal-black sky,
God's natural bedtime story.
Creation preparing for sleep.
Quiet.
Nothing left to say.

The Power of Awe

Do you remember how awe feels?
That breath-catching,
wide-eyed,
jaw-dropping,
thought stopping,
spell-binding,
stunned amazement?
Each time you notice the
beauty, power, and perfection of Creation,
awe takes you by surprise,
arresting the voices in your head
and revealing the absolute divinity of being.
It is one of the many gates of Heaven,
opening right now if you look
intensely at anything.
Are you ready?
Come in.

Birds and Butterflies

Birds don't sing for approval.
Flowers and butterflies don't enter beauty contests.
How do we account for their gratuitous existence?
The answer lies in the experience.
With alluring songs and vibrant colors,
God charms us back into
the holy dance of Creation,
a resplendent alternative
to the raucous circus we call civilization.
Your dance card just arrived,
again.

This Moment

This timeless moment is
perfect, guilt-free, and immaculate.
Don't replace it with a story.
Each new sensation sacred,
don't spoil it with
judgment or dissatisfaction.
The intimate Now invites you into the Garden
while worries and distractions shroud the path.
Is this the life you wanted when you came?
No worries.
A new one starts this instant.

The Secret Garden

Thinking, talking, rushing, planning,
emoting, believing, striving, and reacting
create humanity's action-thriller motion picture
driven by fear, greed, hope, belief, desperation, and pain.
In absolute stillness, all this stops.
Dust settles.
Movie ends.
Peace returns.
The divine world sweettalks the senses
with a thousand brilliant colors
and ridiculous beauty.
In wonder, gratitude and joy,
life slows to the gentle pace of flow.
Welcome back to the secret Garden.
It's been here all along.
You enter through the
gate of stillness.

God Speaks Through Creation

In this space of no plans, no time, and no self,
trees jewel myriad shades of green,
breezes murmur astonishing secrets,
senses sharpen to crystal clarity.
The world brightens with
dazzling beauty and tender Presence.
You are invited through Heaven's trellis
to meet yourself as God,
but leave personal stories outside.
Humans communicate through narratives,
God speaks through Creation.

The Power of Naming

Naming something can change your
feelings and perceptions, even your mind.
What if you named everything God?
Or any word for divinity that awakens
joy, beauty, peace, and love.
Continue naming things for a few minutes.
Notice now you and the world come
alive with those same qualities.
Since the mystic's God is all those things,
you have stepped into the mystical state—
a single field of sacred conscious being.
All God.
All you.

The Teachers of God

An Ode to Matthew Fox

Strolling in my quiet neighborhood,
no squealing cars or human chatter,
I am aware of every sentient presence on the path,
tree, bird, rock, wind,
beings that know things just as they are.
Mystical experience reveals a living divine universe
of joy, beauty and blessing.
And the teachers of God are everywhere!
All things offer their unique lessons
in the University of Creation Spirituality.

Linger in the Sensory Now

Heaven waits in the sensory world
where mystical consciousness reveals
living portraits of light and color,
landscapes so beautiful ugliness cannot exist.
Nature transports us through the
mental veil into a paradise of love,
everything born anew in the transcendent now.
Will you stay for tea?

Cracking Open Perception

I pray that words from these pages will one day
crack open the pristine and perfect realization
that Creation is God's very being.
This revelation will bring unimaginable joy
and endless God-as-Creation experiences.
Pay attention to these emerging moments.
Each is a pearl of great price.
Each is an open door.
Metanoia is not a matter of belief, trust, or faith,
it's about the sanctification of perception.
We did not fall from grace,
we built another world and
walked away.
Come home.

Increase Your Light

Mystical experience is like increasing
the light in a photo on your computer screen
until it shines through everything.
The light is God's consciousness.
In mystical awareness,
reality lights up, too,
its beauty magnified, perfect,
colorfully woven,
a sacred tapestry come to life through
the transparency of God.
This is the other world.

Stillness

Like a sleepy marsh on a lazy summer day,
nothing seems to be happening,
yet the present moment is profoundly alive.
Insects hum, blossoms open, shadows migrate,
waters ripple, fish feed, and decay putrefies
to create a syncretic moment
more miraculous than
anything conceived in a
thought-driven mental world.
Flawless and sublime, it's only known
in stillness.

Lighting the World

One evening,
at dinner with friends,
a subtle radiance suffused
the gossamer screen of my reality.
Colors brightened.
Conversation morphed distant.
Consciousness awoke, fascinated.
It happens all the time.
Pay attention to the presence of light in being.
God shines through the world.

Cracking the World

Filled with bliss,
I skip into the divine world,
Tarot's Fool.
My joy stops mid-diaphragm.
Fearful questions
claw my soul,
tighten around my heart like a noose:
What should I do here?
Am I acting properly?
What if I told that person how
beautiful they were or
hugged the one with the sad eyes?
What if I invited little children
to silly dance with me?
You see the problem here.
There is no place for ecstasy.
It's against the rules.
But perhaps we could agree on a secret signal,
like touching your nose,
taking a deep relaxing breath,
and smiling warmly.
It would be like a special handshake,
only better.
Divine love would shine between faces
and, for an infinite moment,
the World of Man would crack
and break into
happiness.

Inside God's Mind

Step into the divine mind,
the mystical source of reality.
An invocation like,
"I am inside God's mind,"
can take you there.
Be serious and intensely conscious,
the proof is in the perception.
Everything you experience here is God—
breathtakingly beautiful,
palpably sacred
and absolutely perfect.
You stand at the center of Creation,
God's continuous dream
of Heaven on Earth.

Paradise Now

Gentle mornings.
Children's voices.
Friendships.
Family.
Work.
Simplicity.
Sharing.
Love.
Experiencing all this
in sacred consciousness,
is enough,
is Paradise.

God's Now

The tangible experience of God's
consciousness sustains the mystic.
Thoughts, fantasies, ambitions, and worries
vanish in a world of light and beauty.
Every second, God conjures the
divine world through
our shared consciousness.
In God's now,
there are only miracles.

The Power of the Mystical Vision

The mystic's vision is no "woo woo" head-trip.
Its power and clarity literally erase
the illusions miring humanity
in endless conflict and distraction.
Like someone waking from a crazed dream,
you discover, once again, that reality is
sacred, calm, and beautiful.
Wouldn't you rather live here
than in the movie-land
of your head?

So Beautiful

As you sit quietly reading these words,
plans for the day disappear
and original consciousness opens
to the perfection of divine being,
the enchanted world of early childhood
before the tricksters of
competition and improvement
stole the magic.
Can you still see it?
The transcendent beauty
in this very moment,
and this moment,
and this one, too?

May It Be

May you fall in love with the universe,
stand in awe before
its creativity, splendor, and consciousness,
and sense divinity's presence
in every object, being, and moment.
May you allow the universe to
fall in love with you,
enfold you in its tenderness, and
nourish all do you do with joy.
May your awakening announce the
arrival of the sacred world,
erasing hatred, suffering, and war.
As you become God, may it be so.

Exercise

Spend an hour outside.

Sit or walk slowly.

Open all your senses.

*Experience everything as if
for the very first time.*

Practice awe and gratitude.

Remind yourself that this is Creation—

*God in everything and everything in God,
including you.*

Chapter 8. **Serving Life in Apocalyptic Times**

Humanity's Cult of Fantasy

Humanity has become a cult of addictive fantasies.
Movies project false worlds of light and sound
making us laugh, cry, or recoil in horror.
We can walk out any time, but we don't.
Tech wizards create virtual realities to
wrap us in illusory megaverses,
captives in another's imagination.
Politicians, news venues and advertisers
sell stories to inspire, frighten, or manipulate us
into maintaining our frenzied addictions.
Disneyland promises you the happiest place on Earth.
Even physicists tell us perception is an illusion
and reality is empty, though they miss the spiritual
implications of their pronouncements.
We live in multiplying fantasy worlds
while poisoning Mother Earth beneath our feet.
We are snake charmers soon to be
bitten by the snake.
We lost the Garden once before.
If you want to save humanity,
open your senses to the sacred world
exactly where you are.
Come home.

Are You Willing?

When power, greed, and corruption
tear the fabric of life
the human world comes apart.
We instinctively long for the
original holiness of Creation.
It's suddenly so simple.
Parents, visionaries, and the broken
plead to give love another chance.
For a moment, we see how the rapacious ego
blinds us to Eden.
Waking up can halt this madness.
Are you willing?

The Futility of Control

History amply illustrates
the World of Man is not under our control.
We neither comprehend nor master
the problems we create or
the ineffable nature of being.
Activism mostly involves editing
the scenes of our movie, but it's still a movie.
No one knows what's going to happen
in humanity's perpetual psychodrama.
But you can live moment-to-moment,
allowing mystical consciousness to
light your way, one step at a time,
into the divine world.
Understand this:
seeking control is the
failure of awakening.
Live as if everything were God.
Even you.

The Activism of God

Every moment lived consciously in Creation
is God's activism.
And every mystical revelation,
experienced directly, is
God's
incarnation.

Rebalancing the Psyche

Rebalancing the psyche is up to us.
Spending as much time in Heaven on Earth
as we do in the World of Man would
end the race toward
planetary destruction.
Our happiness,
and the birth of a new humanity,
are in our own hands.

Perception as Solution

Nothing matters more than
the perceptual act of
divinizing every single thing
through mystical seeing.
We will no longer harm Creation,
ignore suffering, or start wars
when everything,
including us,
is directly experienced
as God.

Befriending Creation

Find a plant to befriend.
Approach gently with the sincere
intention of friendship.
Greet it as a conscious being,
Complement its beauty and perfection.
Sense its individuality,
needs, feelings, desires, and joys.
Ask it to befriend you as well.
Start a conversation and let friend's
responses come through your imagination.
Take your time.
You are moving into the non-human
community of sacred beings and the
consciousness of Creation.
What is your new friend telling you?

God Expanding

This I know:
Each moment we experience the luminous,
stunningly beautiful, three-dimensional
hologram that is sacred reality,
humanity's consciousness expands a little more into
the transcendent nature of being,
our home before thought, words,
and pretense replaced
God.

I Am

a flea, a fern, a winter's day,
a skyscraper, a cloud,
two sailors marooned at sea,
and the sea itself with creatures too numerous to count.
I am this broken-down old man writing these words.
We are each God behind the mind's illusions.
In "I Am God" consciousness,
divinity thrums through everything.
Not only is the world sacred,
every relationship becomes an alter
of love, worship, and transformation.
This is how we heal the world.

A United Nations of Species

Crows, elephants, gorillas,
all animals are highly intelligent.
While differently endowed, they
possess remarkedly complex languages
and social organizations
that we refuse to honor as equals.
So, too, plants and insects.
These non-human beings pose the
same communication challenge as imaginary
aliens coming to conquer us from other worlds,
yet, paradoxically, we are the conquering enemies here.
Perhaps, one day, in mystical consciousness,
we will transcend our arrogance to seek
respectful relationships with our fellow beings.
Perhaps we create a United Nations of Species
meeting in peace, dignity, and respect,
as equal communities sharing a single world,
and a new Eden.

Eternity Watching

Settling in God-consciousness,
eternal, immortal, outside of time,
liberated from karma and the mortal coil,
I watch the illusions of the collective mind
through the window of eternity,
like an astronaut peering
down on Earth,
stunned by the banality
of beliefs and boundaries, nationalities and wars.
We are the consciousness of the
Cosmos and Creation.
This mystical realization holds
the promise of awakening
and the key to our survival.
We are eternity watching.

Apocalypse and Rebirth

We stand paralyzed before
a hard-barreling train
carrying the massive freight of
warfare, climate disasters, polluted landscapes,
and human desperation.
Its impact—fierce, powerful, terrifying—
already disrupts our lives.
We tremble in the face of
multiplying catastrophes.
Perhaps a new vision will rise from
the marriage of mystical awakening
and Earth wisdom.
Listen: The sacred world is already here,
divine and conscious.
Do you see it?
As humanity's arrogance fails,
open your consciousness to the guidance of
Spirit, ancestors and love.
Get ready to move
from heartbreak and loss to
the new work of Creation.

The Grace of Sacred Art

We enter the world bearing
gifts for Creation
but misplace them in culture's illusions.
We forget why we came.
When Spirit enters creativity,
work becomes sacred art.
The day fills with grace and
everything becomes clear again.

Make Your Occupation Sacred

Every occupation is sacred:
farmer, engineer, dancer, policeman,
poet, parent, surgeon, retiree, astronaut,
wife, husband, friend.
Performed in divine consciousness,
each creates Heaven on Earth for all of us.
We are the answer.

No Wasted Time

Awake in mystical consciousness,
there is no wasted time,
not because you're being industrious,
but because you are part of God
transforming humanity's consciousness.
Every moment in divinity
liberates more God in everyone.

Startled to Awakening

Life is absurd.
Random even.
Especially the bad things—
divorces, terminations, deaths.
Even if we saw them coming,
we wouldn't be prepared.
Cherished beliefs, everyday habits, and social routines
create a reality that puts us to sleep
until something shatters our illusions.
We find God in the broken and unexpected.
Startled by awe, we wake up for a moment,
and then go back to sleep.
What if we didn't?
What if the unfolding apocalypse
brought us to our senses and
we woke from humanity's collective dream to
the always-present divine world?
What if we shed our foolishness and
found the adoration instead?

Please Stay

Earth travels alone in a universe that
cannot support life elsewhere.
Settling on other planets is wildly improbable:
the survival challenges insurmountable,
their locations light years away, and
our tragic flaws inevitably come with us.
Leaving Eden is but a conceit to
avoid facing our ongoing assault on
the only home we have.
We are born of Earth,
made of Earth, sustained by Earth.
Only on Mother Earth can we survive
and learn to love.
To the mystic, the path is clear:
Worship our divine home
or stumble toward annihilation.
We hold the destiny of human life
in our own hands.

Our Spiritual Destiny

As part of divinity, we participate in
its constant fruition.
Its goal is the fullness of
divine consciousness everywhere.
How we proceed is up to us
which is why
"I Am God" may be
the secret theology of
our spiritual destiny.

Find Your Calling

(for my grandchildren)

Wherever you are,
whatever your circumstances,
create your own world
or the world will create one for you,
like a prison you spend a lifetime escaping.
Tis a huge and sacred calling!
Don't let popular beliefs and values,
rip you apart like piranhas.
Instead, conceive a deeply personal world
inspired by the first-hand experience
of love and joy, kindness and beauty.
Immerse yourself in God's consciousness
to discern what matters most at every crossroad.
Finally, over the long decades,
follow your own divinely-lit path,
but walk lightly, for the
sacred world has much to show you
unseen by those who crush it underfoot.
I promise you,
despite life's chaotic ups and downs,
the unique world you create
will be the source of
your greatest happiness,
freeing your gifts for the world,
and leading directly into
Heaven on Earth.

Holy Work

You can feel God,
commune with God,
live in God
and be lived by God
all the time.
It's how we return to Eden
and feel Heaven's embrace.
Humanity's awakening is up to each of us.
Whatever you feel inspired to do in
mystical consciousness is holy work.
Leave the tyranny of
beliefs, values, and social pressures where
your vision is easily corrupted.
Cut the tether.
Let the soul fly free.

Merging

Boundaries are not as rigid as they seem.
In mystical consciousness,
you can merge with anything . . .
a tree, your cat, that stranger,
your deceased father,
one consciousness melding into another
across time and space.
We are always one with everything
separated only by imagined borders,
fear of others, and the ego's
desire to be special.
Let us merge with each other,
with Earth's creatures, the great teachers,
the cosmos and God.
Let us find oneness and rediscover
the Golden Rule, for
we are the same divine star dust
in wildly-individualized wrappers.

Awaken Sacred Consciousness

So far, save-the-world fantasies
have not healed humanity.
Instead, try this:
Be right where you are
with joy, patience, love and generosity.
Here, now, this!
Make your creativity a sacred
offering to the world
but make love the work you do always.
Humanity's hope rests in awakening
"I Am God" consciousness,
everywhere.

Exercise

Falling in love with the Creator as Creation marks the beginning of mystical activism.

We rarely hurt what we adore and love most deeply.

How does experiencing Eden alter your approach to climate change, social justice, war and every day relationships?

What happens inside when it's all God?

Chapter 9. My Experience

The Poetry of Compassion

God comes in surprising disguises.
Today I am a poetry minnow residing in a small pond.
I labor in solitude beneath raging storms.
Ill-equipped to heal humanity's never-ending anguish,
yet I release tiny poetry bubbles to the surface.
What can a minnow possibly achieve in
such foolish occupation?
Compassion.
Have you never faced your soul's
near extinction from trauma and been
brought back to life by another's compassion?
We hold the crying child, tame the fever,
listen to the broken-hearted, feed the starving,
with compassion.
The universe is a living, conscious,
infinitely loving presence.
Each act of compassion
joins us with its all-embracing tenderness that
we instinctively embody to heal self, other, and Earth.
The minnow knows this and does what he can.
He releases poetry bubbles of compassion.
This poem is one of them.

I am This

Condensation on bathroom mirror.
Sunrise across Puget Sound.
Steam rising off coffee
and mist off water.
Birds at the feeder.
Breathing in, breathing out.
Early morning in the
peace of God.
I am this.

Gratitude

Thank you, God, for
being me,
living me,
transforming me.
And all you ask in return is that
I tend the sacred fires
of love-bliss-wonder
burning in my soul.

Step Across the Threshold

A crafty and determined troll
guarded the bridge across the river
to the radiant world.
For decades, I wrestled with
my divided psyche.
On one side, the land of
competition, conflict, and performance.
On the other, the quiet beauty of Creation
with gentle creatures and sacred symbols.
The ego-troll, weaving spells of failure and defeat,
always blocked my crossing.
One day I decided the pain of staying
was too great and
pushed him aside.
The world is bright and beautiful here.
I stepped across the threshold
hoping you might follow.

Fate

Before words depose sacred reality,
children live in a landscape of magic, mystery, and mysticism.
But the day ego takes charge, this miracle is declared boring.
Rules replace wonder, screens replace play, ambition claims the soul.
My four-year old grandson sits under a bush to escape
the social abrasions already taking their toll.
Though I cannot protect him from the fate of growing up,
I know one day he
will find his way home to himself.
I will wait in eternity to welcome him home to me.

The Cremation of Light

As winter's storms nonchalantly
scatter my detritus of days,
a flame of consciousness quickens within.
The portrait of "me" catches fire.
It grows brighter, fueled by
old identities and memories.
Paint cracks, canvass furls,
the conflagration spreads.
Aging cremates from the inside,
incinerating old poses in sacred expectancy,
until my painting,
once nearly complete,
cools to ashes and
I am free.

The Way of Fatigue

I am a water-soaked log,
a great redwood tree felled
by age and winters' storms,
too heavy to lift, too tired to stand,
sinking into primeval forest,
busy now decomposing with the help
of so many little friends.
It feels good.
Thin green tendrils grow from my
rotting core, seeking sunlight.
They will reach fullness
long after my physical being molders
in the dark moist loving earth.
I take comfort knowing the sacrament of decay
nourishes new life in God's eternal cycle.
My time here eases
toward completion.

Consciousness Blossoming

Nourished by the shadowy fertile depth
of mystical being,
a flower blooms in me—
magnificent, unfurling, evolving, conscious.
Dew sparkles on white petals,
fingerprints of the Beloved.
Its presence translates
ordinary life into sacred moments.
Each day I awaken to a new revelation,
each night sepals close around me in sacred embrace
and Heaven leaks into my dreams.
In the flush of transcendent consciousness,
I shed old ways for new.
May death be the most beautiful blossom of all.

Back in the Sea of Love

Today,
I feel the fullness of mystical reality,
rich with God's being,
overflowing with the immense okay-ness,
no questions asked.
And knowing one more goal from
that old villain Ambition
would instantly reverse this rising tide,
I choose to swim in the sea of love
with all the other little fishes.

What the Heart Desires

What does the heart long for?
Romance, family, achievement, service,
power, recognition, wealth?
My heart has visited these many lands but now
mysticism of the very young draws me back,
where consciousness is immediate and
absorbed in wonder.
My poetry celebrates the divine child of my God-Self
whose original light still
shines gently, quietly, bright with joy.
I am returning to the world I knew
seven decades ago—
timeless and enchanting, love-drenched and safe.
Here dwells my heart's desire,
far from the chaotic marketplace of adulthood.
Isn't this why we were born?
Every true calling leads back the original
home we were meant to share.

The Divinity of Being

Everything in Creation
reaches out to me in love,
desiring relationship, delighting in my visit.
It says, "Join me, dance with me, see what I see."
Experiencing my own divine being,
I experience the divinity of all Being.
We are one tribe.

Pulled into Life by Love

In "I Am God" consciousness,
I enter the sensory present.
Become an enlightened monk
sitting quietly in his cell,
book open, unread,
intensely conscious, motionless,
breathing the still moment,
aware of God's presence,
of being God and
God being me,
of God looking out my eyes,
witnessing the dream as it is,
not as John,
not as anybody.
Questions no longer disturb this unity.
I lean back, absorbed in Heaven.
This is it.
Then Oona drops by,
puts her paws on my shoulders
wants to play.
Oh! This is how we live in God.
Pulled into life by love.

Where I Live

In the brilliant, sharply-etched immediacy
of heightened sensory perception,
God's consciousness
awakens, hones, and polishes my world.
I melt in the incomparable beauty of being.
Other worlds where I once sought identity and membership
—organizations, clubs, societies, schools—
fade into a rapidly-retreating past,
scrapbook memories frangible with time,
images with faded meaning.
In this new sacramental existence,
I live again in divinity.

God's Hot Tub

Sinking,
eyes closed,
into God's deep presence within,
it's like settling into a hot tub,
warm, relaxing, and healing.
Joy bubbles up,
silky, all-consuming,
caressing my tired body,
and I disappear in God,
again.

Nature's Priest

Leaving the frenzied coliseum,
I step into the divine world.
Everything I see and feel is God.
I am repeatedly stunned to silence.
For years I denied imminence.
Language nearly stole my ecstasy.
Now that's all there is—
imminence and ecstasy.
No longer enslaved to warrior life,
ordained nature's priest,
I bring you the new world.

What Does My Three-Year-Old Self Say about Life?

Laugh.
Be silly.
Kick the puddle.
God's playing music.
Do Snoopy dances.
Be happy or get off the bus.
Sure, break down once in a while,
then break dance with me.
Watch!
This is how you do it.

Irony

Seeking God through the transcendence of
duality, illusion, and belief,
I traveled mysticism's
myriad paths for decades.
I discovered the intuitions
of sages already imprinted on my soul
and found God being God
everywhere I looked.
Awakening revealed
the completed whole
and I became it.

My God Is a Laughing God

I know this because when I ask a question,
I hear laughter.
Questions are mind puzzles that end in
tangled cat's cradles.
God chuckles,
"Really?"
Now questions evaporate in
love, wonder and joy.

The Tapestry of Being

We come into the world to love,
but fall in love with the wrong world—
the world of ego, belief, fantasy, competition,
the world of illusion.
Love what's beneath the thought world,
the conscious mystery beyond words
which holds all things in perfect unity.
God weaves a sacred tapestry
of exquisite beauty
all around us.
The day I saw this,
walking alone in the desert,
calling out to God,
I dropped to my knees,
wrapped myself in divinity,
and began my life.

Editing

Like every poet,
I return to poems again and again
to find better words, images, and metaphors.
What surprises me is that I often have
no memory of writing them.
Where did they come from?
I think I know.
I polish these pebbles in
divine consciousness like
my father polished
his gem collection in a tumbler.
Like God polishes me.

Illimitable Joy

Illimitable joy
waits deep in my belly,
smolders,
swirls,
churns.
Knowing this,
I draw in my breath,
hold it in awe,
probe for the inner divine
with short tiny breaths,
until . . .
a blazing hot lava of
Love-Bliss-Exhilaration
surges up from God's unfathomable depths.
Wave after wave of spell-bound elation
floods my being, enters my cells, and
awakens the Holy One as me.
We are permeated by the most sublime joy.
When you experience
this fundamental state of existence,
your fear will end,
your life will heal.

And one day,
these poems,
marinated in divinity,
will dissolve humanity's
brittle vase of painted illusions.
On that day,
the world will be new again.

Trusting Mystical Poetry

I trust these poems.
Each fulsome with God's
essence and ecstasy.
Every word,
vibrant and alive,
consecrates
the living divine universe.
God said,
Keep writing,
no doubts, questions, or
expectations.
Oh, Joy upon joy.

Sitting in the Peace of Heaven

I sit quietly in my
gloriously messy office
watching Northwest raindrops
splash puddles and bless
wind-dancing ferns
in early celebration of spring's return.
The bright greens and red tips of
new growth are everywhere!
Muted gray light pours through large windows,
transfigures this cluttered study into
a luminous, super-real, 3D pageant of
photos, art, books, and prized tchotchkes.
Heaven appears through pellucid gloom.
Divine light illumines ancient hands
recording this moment of wonder
as beautiful as me.
I am fulfilled.

Turning Point

My late-life transition into solitude changed me.
Or I changed in need of solitude.
Maybe both.
It happened during the Covid years.
When the pandemic seemed to end,
I could not return to public life.
Presentations exhausted me.
Articles and books exceeded my tired ego.
It seemed my left-brain productivity had caved
into the right-brain's mystical consciousness.
Remarkably, poetry soon poured
from my sequestered psyche,
flourished almost unstoppably,
and still brings me the greatest joy.
I now delight in the poet's exploration of divinity
and my soul now delights in me.

I Am a Revelation

I am an unfolding mystery,
God's consciousness,
awakening inside,
stirring new revelations,
every moment is a surprise,
an opportunity,
a realization.
Creativity never stops in God.
I am a continuing revelation
even to myself.

Exercise

Pick your favorite poem in this chapter.
Read it slowly, out loud, and let it be about you.
What do you notice?
What begins to happen inside and around you?

Chapter 10. **Dream Visitations**

A Rough Night

I dreamt last night of a woman walking out of a muddy river
carrying the stone bust of an ancient god.
She stumbled, almost fell, but pushed on toward shore.
I dreamt last night of an acquisitions editor who excelled
at exploiting creativity for profit
while killing each writer's passion.
I was too tired to argue with her.
I dreamt last night of a snake with wheels
designed by clever computer engineers to
weaponize its mobility.
A wicked gleam flashed in beady eyes as
forked tongue sniffed for prey.
What does all this mean?
We've lost the wisdom of ancient gods
in the muddy waters of civilization, where
passion is squeezed for profit, and cynical experiments
manufacture cyborgs in nature.
The divine feminine stumbles bravely for shore.
Lao Tzu said,
"Muddy water, let stand, becomes clear."
There is no clarity without stillness and
no stillness without peace.
It was a rough night.

I Dreamt Last Night . . .

I dreamt last night of the
life-giving waters of Spirit
flowing back into
scarred, denuded, arid lands
devastated by the dark masculine's ruthless
machine assault on Earth.
Yet there are still places
untouched, rich and fertile.
It's not too late.

I dreamt of two long lines of women,
fierce and determined,
one gathering garden supplies,
the other giving birth,
preparing for the work that lies ahead—
restoring a place for life's return.

I dreamt of an energetic young woman
beginning a career in nursing
idealistic with hope and vision for the future.
I love and celebrate her optimism.

I knew then that we could never go back
to the old masculine.
The patriarchal age must end
or the loam of life dies.

Heaven on Earth is
born, sanctified and replenished
from the feminine spirit,
not won in masculine wars and
male-dominated religions.
Fathers fertilize, support, protect, and strengthen,
but our damaged world heals with
mothers, children, gardens, and the return of the goddess.

Feminine consciousness dwells in each man who
knows and honors this ancient truth:
The way forward is
back to our original home in
Earth's sacred garden.
God reveals the divine world through us.
Holding hands,
Adam and Eve
begin again.

The Chaos of End Times

In last night's dream,
a disabled spaceship hurtles toward Earth.
People wonder what will happen,
where it might crash,
how to prepare.
We don't know when it will hit,
but it will be soon,
a matter of hours or days.
Most dismiss its potential threat.
I am terrified.
God whispers,
Fall to your knees.
Ready your soul for impact.
Humanity's high-flying ego will scatter like
debris in a massive tornado.
You've been drunk on
hubris, fossil fuels, and self-indulgence,
ventured far from the Sacred Earth.
The clock cannot turn back.
Like a massive asteroid,
Shiva rushes toward humanity's folly.
But horror will meld your consciousness
into the holy moment of my arrival.
Be wide awake.
The empire is coming apart in love.
Apocalypse means revelation in Greek.

Guidance from Angels

A silent, stately, powerful angel dressed in white
visited my dreams last night
seeking donations
for a cause she would not discuss.
If you asked her questions, she walked away.
Apparently, it concerned a task from the other world
that cannot be grasped by the ego.
Hundreds of people have joined her movement.
Sensing the importance of the angel's cause,
I decide to donate.
I start to write a check but
can't remember the date.
Then I learn that a big spiritual event is
scheduled for tomorrow.
It calls for
face painting,
sitting in consciousness, and
performing an exercise to identify
an action you could take to help the world.
Then I get it!
You can only join this movement by
forgetting your time-sense,
assuming a transcendent identity,
centering in consciousness, and
using a discernment exercise to uncover your
contribution to gift to Creation.

It's a description of mystical activism!
I decide to attend the event and someone says,
"You're probably a member now."
I laugh out loud. Well of course!
What's the moral?
When an angel comes seeking your help to
heal the world, drop everything,
wake up, and
join her campaign.

Exercise

Enter mystical imagination and call forth your angel.

Ask the angel to describe a sacred contribution you might make for Creation.

Imagine ways you could perform it.

You are now working with angels!

Chapter 11. The Final Season, Dying into God

Trains

Two trains travel opposite routes.
One, boarded excitedly by the frenetic young,
races into the vast imaginal world
of heroic quests and love adventures,
terrifying and tempting,
wild and bold,
designed to reveal each rider's
nascent gifts and destiny
as they rush far from childhood wounds.
The other train, carrying quiet elders,
moves slowly, calmly,
past scenes of moments intensely lived,
long-forgotten successes and failures,
all the way back to beginnings,
to the rise of consciousness and
the first glimpses of the inner life.
Youth seek Heaven out there,
advertised in the fictions of popular belief,
occasionally tasting its joys, but
never satisfied, always onward;
while elders, if they are patient and perceptive,
will find the bliss of Heaven within,
dwelling in original joy
and the timeless peace of presence,

needing nothing more than gentle reminders
of a life fully lived
to bring them safely home to the greater world
they were seeking all along,
its light now leaking
through parting curtains.

For My Family: An Image of Aging

At 78,
I am a dilapidated old jalopy,
bouncing haphazardly along a bumpy dirt road,
kicking up dust, tires low,
fenders dented, gas tank mostly empty,
a snail could go faster.
Sometimes I stop to rest in a field
to warm my metal frame in the sun.
And it's ok.
The clock has stopped.
The race is over.
I no longer do workshops, articles, or books.
With nothing left to accomplish,
I am free to know the world in a new way,
full of magic, miracles and poetry,
even as I may appear useless and irrelevant to others.
But what I love most is sharing the magic I've found
with my children and grandchildren,
in the backyard,
at the park,
eating ice cream cones that
drip down our chins.

The Land of Fairies

How does a waning grandfather serve his brood
as they chase the action and thrills of embodiment?
My sand castle washed away years ago and
now reposes in the heart's ineffable memories,
irrelevant to the newly liberated.
I offer only simple presence—
quiet, gentle, loving.
It's what my grandmother gave me as a boy
sitting on the sunny patio
telling me about fairies.

Seeds from the Spirit World

Sitting together in the dirt,
my four-year-old grandson asked,
"Will you die before me?"
"Yes," I answered, "old people usually die before the young."
"When you die, you go to the spirit world," he pronounced.
"Yes, and I will still love and protect you when I'm gone."
He turned and resumed digging small holes
to plant the seeds we brought back from the park.

The Grace of Age

Like an old clock, I am running down.
I relax into the nature of things,
welcoming the seasons, days, and moments
of the eternal now,
all the while moving with the
conscious frugality of the seasoned old.
You don't conquer aging,
you receive it as a dear friend.
Observing how shockingly-beautiful
autumn leaves float down to
join Creation's yearly celebration of life,
or how great trees tip over after storms,
I sense how life ends.
True being, like the sunrise and the rose,
is natural and effortless.
So, too, is leaving.
Here, now, finally,
I enter flow,
letting go so my
spirit can go where it wants.
It knows the way from here.
And the joy.

Twilight

One day, in the journey of age,
you begin to disappear from
family pictures.
You are fading away
and it's out of your hands.
In twilight years,
we slip from active participant to
distant observer.
Though love never ceases,
we do.
The drama of life becomes a dream,
from which you must awaken.
Another, brighter world, subtly materializes
within your newly transparent consciousness.
It is the opening of your next adventure.
Take your time.
Say your love.
Prepare yourself.
Let go.

Preparing for Death

Before you die,
death subtly signals your
upcoming departure with
infirmities, losses, social invisibility.
With dreams of traveling to new places.
You are being prepared
to leave the world you
never fully understood.
One day you startle with the realization
that you've already boarded the night train.
It's beginning to move.
With a jolt of realization,
your new journey
begins.

Getting Ready

Old age asks you to trade
self for soul
and performance
for God.
Heaven is the embodiment
of love's purpose on Earth—
full immersion in God's joy, love, and being.
Its silky consciousness seeps into
our own as we
ready ourselves for departure.

Death

is when this
version of you ends
but soul continues to
a land of
new adventures.

Dying

No guilt.
No regret.
No judgment.
You will be welcomed with love.
I assure you,
it will be a grand celebration.

How We Leave

If we live long enough,
age will ravage body and mind,
steal words, identity, memories, agency,
even our story and place in the world.
We become wobbly stick figures,
wondering how death will arrive,
like children with
hands over their eyes in the scary dark.
Yet our final dreams are always celebratory—
a sacred marriage, wonderful banquet, new journey,
budding tree, final graduation, or joyous homecoming.
My unraveling will be a gift to God,
surrendering my "Velveteen Rabbit" body
in gratitude and appreciation.
Whether our final approach be
graceful or turbulent,
the end is inevitably divine—
God wrapping body and soul
in a garment of light for the next world.
As the light pours in,
feel the body's weightlessness.
Spread your wings.
Let go.

Crossing Over

Wrinkly hands, gray beard, and sagging eyelids
fashion the beautiful disguise I will discard
dancing across the bridge.

A Banquet of Wonder

Looking out over the Sound,
I watch geese muscle valiantly across
the wide pale sky in yearly migration,
fulfilling ancient instincts
to survive, mate, raise their young,
and one day disappear.
I was once like that,
loving my work,
the pleasures of an ageless body,
and the gaggle of little ones we taught to fly.
But aging's contemplative consciousness
now asks me to surrender the middle journey,
quiet my busy mind,
and comprehend eternity,
even as my body pursues the same destiny
as the geese.
I relax into the grace of being.
Awakened senses greet
the sacred mystery at every turn.
Filled with gratitude and joy,
I join old friends in a banquet of wonder.

Aging into Simplicity

Old age simplifies life.
With less to do, fading ambition, and time running out,
we are surprised to discover a world
that is sensory and fresh,
fascinating, timeless and alive,
a realm of simple meals,
glowing sunsets,
hearty laughter,
rain on window panes.
Hard edges and sharp boundaries
soften into quilted beauty.
This world forgotten since childhood
is home now, fragranced with
intimations of the
coming transcendence.

The Dandelion Way

A time arrives in old age when
memories feel like fading attachments
and the future portends only the heavy freight
of worry, loss, and what-if's.
I choose the Dandelion Way.
Swept up in swirling winds of awakening,
I liberate dancing florets of insight and joy,
seeding humanity's mystical garden one last time,
and return my body's borrowed loam to Creation.
I will be released one day by the
sudden breath of God.

Exercise

Write a thoughtful, tender and hopeful poem about your own eventual aging. Let it reveal a new perspective on the work of this season and the life beyond.

Chapter 12. **Closing Poems**

If

If you're struggling with the world,
you're ensnared in humanity's
high-stress technicolor dream.

If anything is more important than
divine consciousness,
you risk betraying the life
given you.

If you are lost in thought,
You are indeed lost.

If you are still looking for God,
you have forgotten who you are.

If religious beliefs comprise your sole
relationship with the divine,
your awakening is postponed.

If you think God will be found in
some future time, place, or practice,
you never melt in divinity.

If others' beliefs shape or control yours,
you share their prison cell.

If you are driven by rage, hate,
cruelty, or judgment,
you create hell.

Meditate on these principles.
Step through the door of consciousness.
Set yourself free.

Shooting Arrows at the Moon

You may wonder why I write so many poems.
Not that I have much choice, they just keep coming,
but what's the point?
Each poem is a new arrow
shot at the moon.
Though it will never hit its target,
its secret goal is the reflected
light of God.
Keep aiming
until you find its source
inside you.
That's the point.

You Are a Prophet of Transformation

I embrace God's visionary power.
You inherited that power, too.
Like me, you are a prophet of transformation.
Exchange thought for Presence,
intensify enlightened seeing,
and every path leads into Heaven on Earth.
What should you do?
Follow your path.

You Already Know

every insight and revelation
contained in these pages.
You came with them but forgot.
I write theses verses to remind you
of your own wisdom.
Wake up.
Live what you know.

Keep Reading

The hypnotic power of *maya* is so great
that these revelations need to be
read over and over
until its spell finally breaks.
Their lucid transparency,
removes spiritual cataracts that conceal
your soul's original vision.
Learn to see again through
God's eyes.

The Final Irony

You are God dreaming.
The way to know this is to wake up.

Exercise

Keep these poems nearby.

Faced with a new question or issue, randomly open the book to any page and seek the poem or line that speaks to it.

May Divinity Rising become a trusted source of personal revelation.

www.ingramcontent.com/pod-product-compliance
Lightning Source LLC
Chambersburg PA
CBHW071958220426
43662CB00009B/1176